Wales Coast Path: South Wales Coast

Text: *Dennis Kelsall*
Series editor: *Tony Bowerman*
Photographs: *Dennis Kelsall, © Crown copyright (2022) Visit Wales, Vale of Glamorgan Council/www.visitthevale.com, Alex Edwards/ Porthkerry Country Park, Tony Bowerman, Alamy, Dreamstime, Shutterstock*

Design: *Carl Rogers*

© Northern Eye Books Limited 2022

Dennis Kelsall has asserted his rights under the Copyright, Designs and Patents Act, 1988 to be identified as the author of this work. All rights reserved.

This book contains mapping data licensed from the Ordnance Survey with the permission of the Controller of Her Majesty's Stationery Office. © Crown copyright 2022. All rights reserved. Licence number 100047867

Northern Eye Books

ISBN 978-1-908632-31-9

A CIP catalogue record for this book is available from the British Library.

Cover: *Nash Point (Walk 5)*

Important Advice: The routes described in this book are undertaken at the reader's own risk. Walkers should take into account their level of fitness, wear suitable footwear and clothing, and carry food and water. It is also advisable to take the relevant OS map with you in case you get lost and leave the area covered by our maps.

Whilst every care has been taken to ensure the accuracy of the route directions, the publishers cannot accept responsibility for errors or omissions, or for changes in the details given. Nor can the publisher and copyright owners accept responsibility for any consequences arising from the use of this book.

If you find any inaccuracies in either the text or maps, please either write to us or email us at the addresses below. Thank you.

First published in 2016. This edition 2022

Northern Eye Books Limited
Northern Eye Books, Tattenhall, Cheshire CH3 9PX
Email: tony@northerneyebooks.co.uk

For sales enquiries, please call 01928 723 744

www.northerneyebooks.co.uk
www.walescoastpath.co.uk

Instagram: @wales_coast_path

Twitter: @WalesCoastUK
@Northerneyeboo

Facebook: @WalesCoastGuidebooks

Printed in the EU by Latitude on woodland-friendly FSC stock

Contents

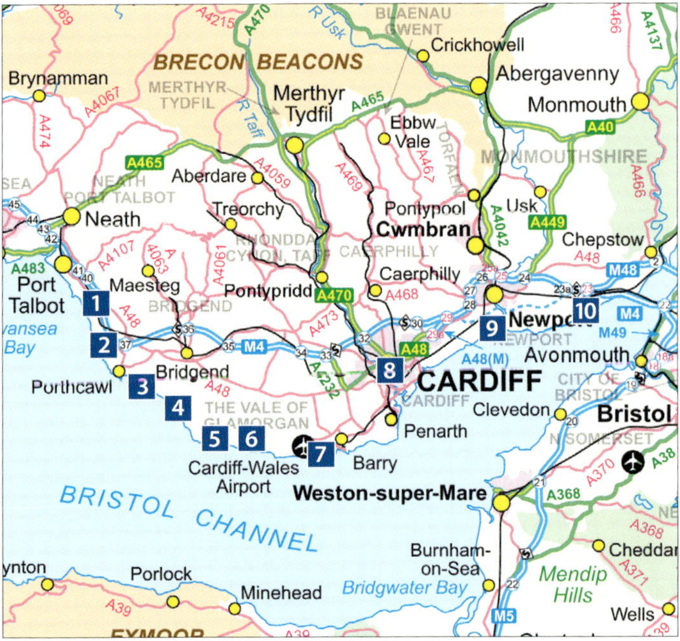

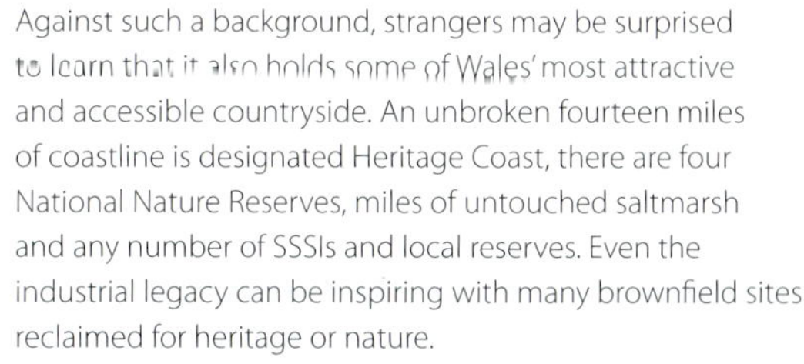

The powerhouse of Wales

During the late 18th and 19th centuries, South Wales exploded as a major industrial centre of the Empire. Its iron, steel and stone were the building blocks of enterprise and Welsh coal fuelled ships and railways across the world, all making the docks amongst the busiest ever known. Although much of that industry has disappeared, the south remains Wales' economic and administrative heart and is home to more than half its population.

Against such a background, strangers may be surprised to learn that it also holds some of Wales' most attractive and accessible countryside. An unbroken fourteen miles of coastline is designated Heritage Coast, there are four National Nature Reserves, miles of untouched saltmarsh and any number of SSSIs and local reserves. Even the industrial legacy can be inspiring with many brownfield sites reclaimed for heritage or nature.

Banded limestone strata at Nash Point on the Glamorgan Heritage Coast

South Wales Coast

The past two centuries have wrought more change on South Wales than any other section of the country's coast. Until the end of the 18th century, Swansea, Barry and even Cardiff were just small ports, though their ships traded far and wide. The industry of iron and coal changed things forever but most of the coast and its immediate hinterland were left unspoiled and elsewhere, nature has reclaimed some of what was taken. The coast is one of extreme contrasts, ranging from great dune systems through sheer cliffs to miles of coastal saltmarsh. Nowhere is far from a delightful stretch overlooking the sea, with fine views, nature and heritage all around.

"[*of Swansea*]… an ugly, lovely town … by the side of a long and splendid curving shore. This sea-town was my world."

Dylan Thomas, *Reminiscences of Childhood*

TOP 10 Walks: South Wales Coast

FAR-REACHING VIEWS, A STUNNING DIVERSITY OF LANDSCAPE and the richness of the area's heritage are all explored in these ten short, circular walks. From vast dune systems packed with wildlife to miles of dramatic limestone cliffs, it's a fascinating area. All but one of the walks have a footprint on the coast, whilst the other steps back for the view from the verdant hills behind. Visiting at least one place of outstanding interest, none of the walks are difficult and each passes somewhere for refreshment or has a friendly pub close to hand.

Nash Point &
St Donats
page 30
Llantwit Major
page 36

Porthkerry
Country Park
page 40

Cardiff Bay
page 46

Nash & Uskmouth
page 52

Redwick
page 58

Victorian Margam Castle dominates Margam Country Park

Margam Country Park

Although an inland walk, there are superb coastal views and a good chance of seeing the herd of fallow deer

What to expect:
Generally good tracks but with one steeper climb

Distance/time: 5.6 km/3½ miles. Allow 1½ to 2 hours

Start: Margam Country Park car park (charge) off A48, south east of Margam

Grid ref: SS 801 860

Map: Ordnance Survey Explorer 165 (Swansea)

After the walk: Charlotte's Pantry in castle courtyard SA13 2TJ | 01639 881635 OR The Twelve Knights, Margam Road, Port Talbot SA13 2DB | 01639 882381

Walk outline

The route begins through the country park, passing the Victorian castle and around the foot of an ancient hillfort to continue up Cwm Philip. Later climbing the hillside out of the valley, the landscape opens up to reveal splendid views back to the coast. There is then a pleasant stretch across open deer park before the path falls back to the castle, visitor centre and gardens.

Margam Country Park

With origins in a 12th-century Cistercian abbey the estate was acquired at the Dissolution by the Rice Mansels, whose descendants developed the 19th-century docks and industry of Swansea and Port Talbot. The 'castle' was begun in 1830 near an 18th-century orangery that had replaced an earlier Tudor mansion. Surrounded by formal gardens and a deer park, it remained the family home until requisitioned during the Second World War. The hall gradually became derelict, but following its purchase by Glamorgan County Council in 1973, the house has gradually been restored and is partially open during the summer, while the grounds can be visited all year round.

Ornamental urn

Rhododendrons

The Walk

1. From the **entrance kiosk**, walk forward along the main drive, bearing right to wind above a car park. The drive continues below the **garden terraces** fronting the house to a junction by a **miniature railway**. Keep ahead to a second junction, there bearing right to follow a broad track up to a **high gate in a deer fence**.

In 1730 the estate passed to the Talbot branch of the family. They preferred their house at Penrice but developed Margam as a pleasure garden, eventually demolishing the ancestral Tudor house in 1786 to make way for a magnificent orangery, which is reputedly the longest in Britain. Christopher Rice Mansel Talbot (who pioneered the development of the docks and coastal industry) brought the family back to Margam, building the 'castle' and extending the gardens but demolishing Margam village in the process. He planted more than 5,000 trees and shrubs, the work keeping a team of eighteen or more gardeners busy.

2. Through that, climb ahead between rhododendrons to a fork. Take the left branch, indicated by a green arrow,

© Crown copyright and/or database right 2016. All rights reserved. Licence number 100047867

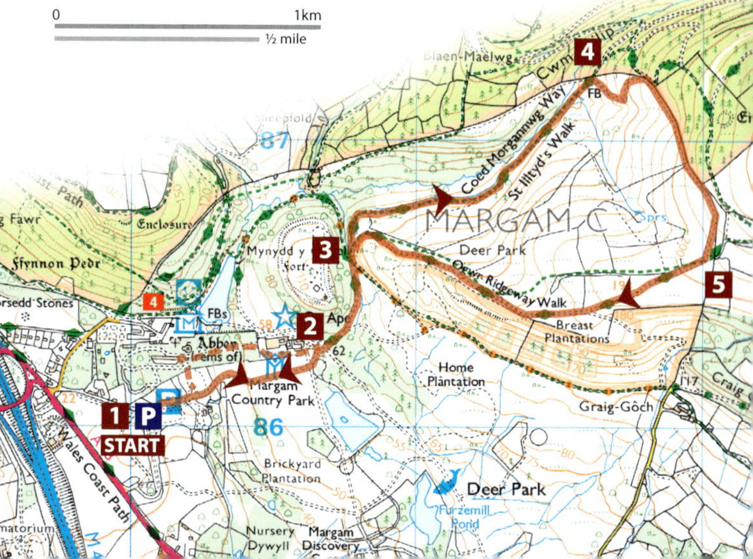

The atmospheric ruins of medieval Margam Abbey

which skirts the foot of a steep hill, the site of an **Iron Age hillfort**.

3. Reaching another junction beneath a large beech tree, keep ahead with the main trail to a second junction. Bear right, still following green arrows. *Felling and replanting as the trees reach maturity as well as rhododendron control are creating changing views across the foot of Cwm Philip to Cwm Maelwg.*

Rounding a bend into **Cwm Philip**, pass through another deer gate to rise pleasantly along a more open valley side above the bubbling **stream** below.

Amongst the deciduous trees of the woods are sweet chestnut, beech, alder and oak, which attract birds such as jay, nuthatches, tree creepers, thrushes and blackbirds; you may also see ravens and buzzards circling above.

The understorey and clearings are rich in wildflowers; look out for carpets of bluebells, tall spikes of foxgloves and the delicate flowers of violets. In addition to the deer, there are many smaller mammals too; squirrels and foxes are commonplace and brown hares roam the more open ground.

The magnificent Orangery, fronted by palms and ornamental urns

4. Approaching a gate and stile back into forest, leave the main trail for a path off on the right. After winding steeply up the hillside it settles beside a **stone boundary wall.** Beyond a deer gate, the gradient eases, soon cresting the hill where the view expands across Swansea Bay to Gower. *Closer to, you might well catch sight of the park's deer herds.*

5. The way eventually descends to a waypost, where a crossing path enters the park over a **high ladder stile** by a gate. Follow it away from the wall along the crest of a gently descending ridge, aiming for the conical wooded hill of the Iron Age fort. Beyond a viewpoint at the **Pulpit Stone**, the path tends to the landward side of the ridge, the prospect across the bay exchanged for one back across Cwm Philip. Shortly dropping into rhododendron thicket, the path returns you to the junction by the beech tree (Waypoint **3**).

Turn left, retracing your outward steps to the **boundary deer gate** (Waypoint **2**). Instead of returning directly to the car park, now keep ahead towards the castle, where the **courtyard** contains a **café, gift shop** and **exhibition** about the park's history. Walking beyond the courtyard entrance, pass through a gate into the **terrace garden**. Leave by steps dropping from the western façade, which lead towards the **abbey ruins** behind the **church**.

Beyond is the magnificent **orangery** overlooking more floral displays, while a path on the left leads back past a car park to the **entrance kiosk** to complete the walk. ◆

Deer, deer, deer

Three herds of deer roam the park: fallow, red and Père David deer. Of the three, only red deer are native to Britain and are seen mainly in Scotland, the South West and East Anglia. They were introduced to the park around 15 years ago. More recent are the rare Chinese Père David herd, known in the West only since 1865. Fallow deer on the other hand were introduced to Britain by the Normans as a game animal and roam widely across Britain.

Dense reedbeds fringe Kenfig Pool

Kenfig Burrows

Freshwater lake, dunes, woodland and beach brought together in a single, superb walk

Distance/time: 6.5 km/4 miles. Allow 1½ to 2 hours

Start: Car park at Kenfig National Nature Reserve

Grid ref: SS 801 810

Map: Ordnance Survey Explorer 151 (Cardiff & Bridgend)

After the walk: Prince of Wales pub (½ mile to the north towards Mawdlam), Ton Kenfig CF33 4PR | 01656 740356

Walk outline

The first stage of the walk is around the east and northern shores of Kenfig Pool, visiting a water's-edge bird hide before striking off across the burrows to the coast. Wander onto the beach or stick with the coast path until it is time to head back across the dunes to the car park.

Kenfig Burrows

Kenfig Pool is the largest freshwater lake in Glamorgan and was once believed to be bottomless, although in fact it is barely 12 feet. It formed during the 13th-15th centuries, when a prolonged spate of storms and high winds began moving the coastal dune bank, blocking streams that formerly flowed out to the sea. The dunes also buried the old town of Kenfig and only the ruin of its castle remains, a mile to the north.

Today, the dunes, pool and surrounding wetlands are rich in wildflowers, some quite rare. The water also attracts many migratory birds, particularly during the winter months.

Walking in the Burrows

Dune pansy

The Walk

1. Leaving the rear of the **car park**, a path heads almost due west towards **Kenfig Pool**. Keep going as tarmac gives way to sand, shortly passing a small **picnic area** before meeting the lake shore.

2. Swing right on a path over **low sand hills** covered in bracken and burnet rose to a stile. The way continues at the water's edge beside flower-rich meadows, where clouds of blue damselflies. dance above swathes of flag iris that flower in early summer.

Keep going from stile to stile, eventually passing the **ruin of a building** out in the water. Bear away from the lake to reach yet another stile.

3. Follow an initially broad track to the left, shortly passing between the tip of the lake and another **small pool**. Keep going along a **boardwalk** that leads to a **bird hide** overlooking the reedy shores of the lake.

It is ironic that Kenfig Pool, now a nature reserve, was once managed for sport.

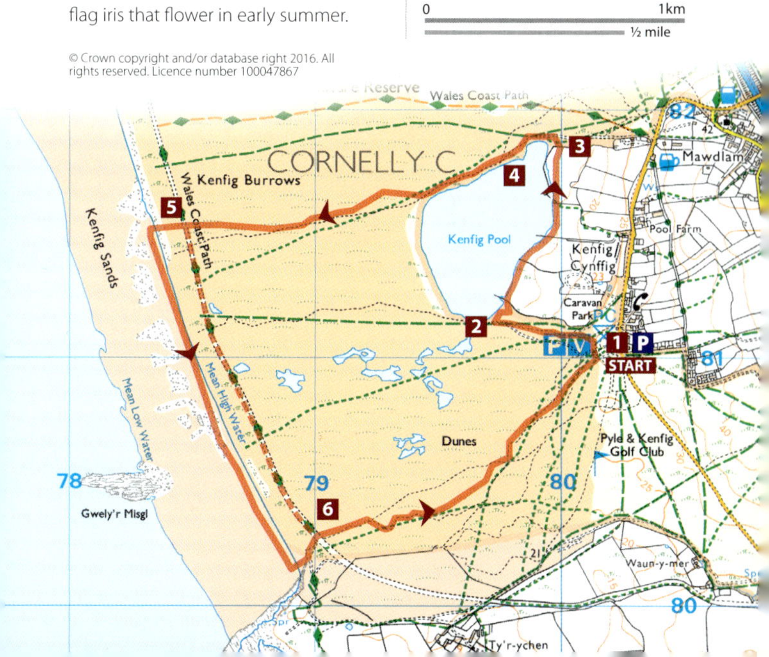

When Thomas Mansel Talbot inherited the Margam estate in the 18th century, he planted willows and reeds around the shore and raised an island in the lake to encourage breeding wildfowl for his shooting. He also stocked the lake with pike and other fish and kept a boat on the water from which to fish. Although his island has sunk, the wetland lake borders still attract numerous birds including coot, teal, tufted ducks and pochards. From time to time, whooper and Bewick's swans put in an appearance and in winter there is sometimes a glimpse of the elusive bittern.

4. Return partway along the boardwalk before leaving left on a path that is initially sometimes wet as it follows the northern shore of Kenfig Pool.

The only visible evidence of the medieval town of Kenfig is the sparse ruin of a Norman castle on the northern edge of the dunes. Under the castle's protection, it grew to be one of the largest in the area, hosting a market that traded in farm produce and leather goods. Change came during the 14th century when a climatic shift to high winds and exceptional tides destabilised the coastal dunes, which then began to

The dunes at Kenfig Burrows are a priceless natural habitat

creep inland, gradually smothering the town and its surrounding fields. Despite many attempts to stem the shift, the village was finally abandoned around the 1470s, with the church dismantled stone by stone and re-assembled at nearby Pyle.

Shortly reaching a fork, branch right, the path soon becoming more distinct and settling along a roughly westerly course across the dunes. The terrain alternates between wetland and sandy areas, undulating gently on for about ½ mile/800 metres. Keep with the main trail as it then swings sharply right and left, eventually meeting a broad, crossing track, the **Wales Coast Path**.

5. The way lies to the left, either along the track or on the beach that lies just beyond the dunes, a great swathe of sand backed by a bank of cobbles that lies just beyond the dunes. When the water is out, the strand offers easy walking, but the cobbles at high tide are a far less attractive proposition.

If you've opted for the shore, walk for almost a mile/1.6 kilometres to the rocks at **Sker Point**. Leave where the rocks begin below a **lifeguard station**, doubling back inland along a broad track to a junction. If you kept to the coast path, follow it south for a mile/1.6kilometres to the same point.

6. Cross (or turn left) to follow a broad, **sandy track**, which winds inland through the dunes. Eventually, a bridleway joins from the left. Keep forward, but after a few paces the track forks. The bridleway continues ahead, but you should bear left with the footpath, which winds on through the dunes back to the car park to complete the walk. ♦

Rare plants amongst the dunes

In 2009, a new orchid hybrid was discovered amongst the dunes, a cross between the southern marsh and fragrant marsh orchids. Other rarities include the fen orchid and autumn lady's tresses as well as the more familiar pyramidal, bee and common spotted orchids. There are concentrations of marsh and broad-leaved helleborine too. Other wildflowers to be seen across the reserve are autumn gentian, twayblade, stinking iris and sea holly.

The sand hills at Merthyr-mawr are the highest in northern Europe

Merthyr-mawr Warren

A superb walk exploring the highest sand dunes in northern Europe, used as a location for the film Lawrence of Arabia

What to expect:
A mixture of woodland, thicket, dune and beach walking

Distance/time: 10.5 km/6½ miles. Allow 2½ to 3 hours

Start: Public car park by Candleston Castle

Grid ref: SS 871 772

Map: Ordnance Survey Explorer 151 (Cardiff & Bridgend)

After the walk: The Jolly Sailor, Church Street, Newton CF36 5PD | 01656 782403

Walk outline

After exploring the ruin of Candleston Castle, the path climbs through woodland around Merthyr-mawr Warren, eventually dropping out at the edge of Newton. The way winds through the village, passing the Jolly Sailor and the church before heading back to the Ogmore estuary. The final leg turns up beside the river and into the trees to find the car park.

Merthyr-mawr Warren

Merthyr-mawr, Kenfig and Crymlyn burrows are parts of a single dune system that once extended around the full sweep of Swansea Bay. Although now interrupted by docks, industrial development and housing, they remain an impressive feature, with the hills at Merthyr-mawr extending over 1¼ square miles and rising to over 200 feet — the highest in northern Europe.

Driven by the prevailing winds and breached by occasional storms, they constantly change and are the youngest of all geological formations, supporting a wide diversity of habitats. Over 300 plant species have been recorded, while invertebrates include the rare grizzled skipper butterfly and the great green bush cricket, the largest in Britain.

Nearing the Ogmore Estuary

Vipers bugloss

The Walk

1. A broad sandy track winds north from the **car park** through trees. Continue for ¼ mile/400 metres until the track begins to rise.

2. Leave beside a **National Nature Reserve** sign on the left, climbing through wood and scrub to a fork. Bear right, breaking from the trees to a second junction. Go through a kissing gate on the left, the path running on beside a wall within the woodland fringe. At the next junction, keep left, later passing through another gate. The path continues at the edge of the dunes, passing through two more gates. Keep right as a path then joins from the left, shortly encountering a **National Nature Reserve board** beside a cross path at the edge of open ground, an old rifle range.

3. Turn right into trees. A sharp pull leads to a junction at the top edge of the wood. Go left, descending gently within the tree fringe and keeping ahead past barrier post as the way then levels toward houses. Continue behind them to emerge onto a street.

4. Take the footpath opposite, crossing another street and finally emerging onto **Church Street**. Follow it right and then bend left around the perimeter of an allotment to reach the **Jolly Sailor**.

5. Leave left opposite the pub and walk past the church entrance, joining a lane dropping across the **village green**. Keep with the ongoing street to the end of the houses and bear off left towards a **car park by the beach**.

A couple enjoying the view from Ogmore across Merthyr-mawr beach

6. Follow a track left through the dunes behind the beach. After a mile/1.6 kilometres, at a waymark just beyond the tide-washed outcrop of **Black Rocks**, if you have not already done so, move right to continue at the head of the beach past the **Merthyr-mawr Warren**.

7. Approaching the **Ogmore estuary**, the path turns in to follow the river upstream, soon sweeping in around the head of a marshy apron. After ½ mile/800 metres, turn away from the river along the broad channel of a usually-dry stream bed. Entering woodland, the path winds on, shortly leading you back to the car park to complete the walk. ♦

Candleston Castle

Candleston is said to take its name from the de Cantilupes, who took over the manor in the 12th century. The castle, in reality a fortified house, dates from the 14th century. Although the drifting sands gradually smothered its coastal farmlands, the house escaped engulfment by being sited on higher ground. Much altered, the building had decorative crenellations added before it was finally abandoned in the 19th century.

The honey-hued limestone cliffs above Traeth Mawr, Southerndown

Ogmore & St Brides Major

A taste of the Glamorgan Heritage Coast, looping back across pleasant farmland and an inland dune system

Distance/time: 11 km/6¾ miles. Allow 2½ to 3 hours

Start: Large coastal car park at Ogmore-by-Sea

Grid ref: SS 861 755

Map: Ordnance Survey Explorer 151 (Cardiff & Bridgend)

After the walk: Tea bar at Dunraven Bay, OR The Pelican in her Piety pub, Ogmore Rd, Bridgend CF32 0QP (on the B4524 northeast of Ogmore-by-Sea) | 01656 880049

Walk outline

The first leg of the walk follows the cliffs of the Heritage Coast past Southerndown to Dunraven Bay, a justifiably popular beach tucked into the lee of a high promontory. Heading inland past the Heritage Coast Centre, the route climbs through Slade Wood and across the fields to St Brides Major. After a short walk through the village, there's another stretch across fields before dropping to the River Ogmore along the dry limestone valley of Pant y Cwteri. The final stretch to the sea offers fine views across the river and its estuary.

Ogmore-by-Sea

Ogmore-by-Sea's name is said to derive from 'eog', the Welsh for salmon; the river was once renowned as one of the finest salmon rivers in South Wales. Although pollution drove them away, the last thirty years have seen the fish returning to their old breeding grounds. Two hundred years ago, the place was little more than a scattering of farms centred around Sutton Quarries where fine limestone had been cut since the Middle Ages. Soft enough to saw when freshly cut, it hardened with weathering and was reputedly used in the Palace of Westminster.

Overlooking Traeth Mawr

Salmon

The Walk

1. Skirt the seaward edge of the car park to a gate at the southern tip. Continue along a grassy shelf above a rocky platform backing the beach, a vantage exploited by fishermen at high tide. After some ½ mile/800 metres, the path rises inland along a **shallow gully**.

2. Approaching the road, swing sharp right beside a stone wall and head back towards the cliffs, which give a fine retrospective view past Tusker Rock to Porthcawl and Gower. The path is soon turned inland again by another **deep gully**, but resumes its cliff-top course behind **West Farm Barn**.

The fourteen miles between Porthcawl and Aberthaw has been designated Heritage Coast, incorporating the dunes of Merthyr-mawr and the fine run of cliffs beyond Ogmore-by-Sea that attract a variety of birds including fulmars, peregrines and choughs.

3. After ½ mile/800 metres, approaching a wall, leave through a gate and **small car park** onto the lane, which drops to a car park at **Dunraven Bay**. Take care if you use the path running above unguarded cliffs.

Wave-cut limestone strata curving into the sea on Traeth Mawr

The apron of beach below has extensive clumps of honeycomb reef formed by colonies of small worms, while the rock pools contain molluscs, crabs and sea anemones.

4. Turn inland up the lane opposite the car park. Beyond the **Heritage Coast Centre**, keep forward across grass to a gate, from which a path rises at the edge of **Slade Wood**. Ignore a permissive path leaving through a wall gap and instead, swing left through the thick of the wood to a stile.

5. Walk ahead by the left field boundary, winding through the corner to continue with the hedge on your right. In the next two fields, stick with the left hedge. Then, over a stile go right to a gate. Cross a final small field to a stile near the far-left corner and walk out to a lane opposite the **Farmers Arms**.

6. Turn left past **Pitcot Pool** (Pwll y Mêr), a local nature reserve and then bear right with the main lane through the village of **St Brides Major**.

Before the introduction of piped water, the village relied on wells and springs. Two

Distinctive bands of limestone lain down in an ancient sub-tropical sea

survivors are passed during the walk; one by the Heritage Coast Centre at Dunraven and another in the fold of Pant y Cwteri. Pitcot Pool was also a source of water and a decorative handpump has been erected beside it to commemorate a well that was lost when the road was widened.

Reaching a junction, turn left and then keep right past 12th-century **St Bridget's Church** to head uphill out of the village. *The Norman church is dedicated to St Bride or Bridget, a 5th-century Irish abbess who founded several nunneries including one at Kildare. She is said to have sailed across the sea to Wales on a piece of turf and performed many miracles. Inside the church are several funerary monuments including a 13th-century incised slab depicting Sir Johan le Botiler of Dunraven in full armour.* Over a cattle grid, bear left at a fork by the base of an **ancient cross**.

7. Approaching a farm, cross a wall stile left of the gate and walk on beside the right-hand field edge. Over a stile in the top-right corner, continue by the left hedge in successive fields, ultimately emerging onto a track.

8. Walk over a grass triangle towards a lane, but then bear right to remain with the right-hand fence. Ignore a grass track off right then curve right to descend along the deepening fold of **Pant y Cwteri**. Keep going as another path later joins from the left to emerge at the bottom onto the **B4524**.

9. Cross to the **dunes** opposite, bearing left to pick up a path above the **River Ogmore** and follow it down to the estuary to complete the walk. ♦

Limestone fossils

The cliffs along the Glamorgan Heritage Coast are formed of layered beds of Carboniferous limestone overlain with shales, conglomerates and Jurassic lias; the layers vary in colour through grey and white to a rich honey hue. The Carboniferous limestone was formed over millions of years from the skeletons of countless microscopic animals living in a warm, shallow sea. Look out for the fossils of ancient sea creatures, including ammonites, corals and sponges.

Nash Point has been shaped by the timeless wash of the sea

Nash Point & St Donat's

A lovely stretch of coastal walk that includes a pair of light-houses and two interesting churches

Distance/time: 7.5 km/4¾ miles. Allow 2 to 2½ hours

Start: Coastal car park at Nash Point (charge)

Grid ref: SS 916 683

Map: Ordnance Survey Explorer 151 (Cardiff & Bridgend)

After the walk: The Horseshoe Inn, Marcross, Llantwit Major CF61 1ZG | 01656 890568

Walk outline

The walk begins above coastal cliffs, passing Nash's twin lighthouses and descending to the head of a beach below St Donat's College. Climbing through woodland beyond, the route then turns inland to the lane and follows it into the village. The way continues through the college grounds to St Donat's Chapel before heading across the fields to Marcross, where there is another church. The final leg follows Marcross Brook down a delightful valley to the coast.

St Donat's and Nash Point

The village of St Donat's is centred upon an ancient castle, more lately taken over as an international college, and although the grounds are private, there is a path across giving access to the old church. The way to it lies along a particularly impressive stretch of Heritage Coast, passing a pair of 19th-century lighthouses, built to warn shipping of the dangerous shoals and reefs off Nash Point. There is access to the beach at the foot of Cwm Marcross below the car park and also by a steep path down the cliffs to a tiny cove immediately beyond St Donat's.

Nash Point lighthouse

Fulmar

Heading along the cliffs from Nash Point towards the lighthouses

The Walk

1. Follow the drive beyond the car park, which leads past the **Nash lighthouses**. Over a stile beyond the second light, the path continues above crumbling cliffs for another ¾ mile/1.2 kilometres. *There are some splendid views, but occasionally, wind-sculpted thorn banks obscure the prospect.*

2. Approaching **St Donat's**, the path crosses a stile and descends through a grove of stunted sycamore to a **concrete quay**. Over a stile towards the far end, follow a path up into the trees. After briefly emerging at the edge of fields, the way continues within more cliff-top woodland, where a crossing path drops steeply to the rocky beach. The onward route, however, lies ahead, exiting the trees through a kissing gate.

3. Go left beside a couple of fields to a lane and follow it left into the **village**. Although the church is signed through **St Donat's College** on the bend, this may be closed, in which case, continue with the lane to the next entrance, which is a public footpath.

St Donat's Castle was transformed into a grand residence by the American newspaper magnate William Randolph Hearst in 1925. However, Hearst's fortunes waned and before he could sell the castle, it was requisitioned for the war effort. In 1962 it was bought by Atlantic College, which today attracts students from around the world.

Follow the drive down to a junction and swing off right past the visitors' car park, descending beside the castle wall to **St Donat's Church**.

St Donat's Bay served as a landing for early Celtic missionaries, spreading the Christian faith along the coasts of western Europe. An early chapel was dedicated to St Gwerydd, a 5th-century Welsh saint, although local legend tells of an even earlier church, established by the daughter of Caractacus in the 1st century. The Normans founded the castle shortly after their arrival in Glamorgan during the 11th century, building the present church at the same time and dedicating it to St Donat, a patron saint of seafarers. Inside are copies of 16th-century painted panels depicting the Stradling family, who held St Donat's for more than 400 years, and an interesting lectern with a revolving book holder supported on a figure of St John the Evangelist.

Nash Point's twin lighthouses mark dangerous offshore shoals

4. Return briefly up the drive before leaving left on a rough track into trees. Soon narrowing to a path it rises along a narrow, wooded valley. Through gates at the top, walk past converted barns to a fork.

5. Taking the left branch, leave after a few paces over a stile on the left. Walk around the property to a stile and head away by the right wall. Over another stile in the corner, strike half-left towards the next farm, following a fence across a final field to come out onto a track.

6. Going right, leave the **farm** along a narrow lane. After some 200 metres, turn off through a gate on the left and follow the right boundary to a stile. Head out towards the right-hand corner of a small wood, emerging beyond onto a lane in **Marcross**. The **pub** lies a short distance to the right.

7. The way back, however, is to the left, passing a **small church**. You can simply follow the lane back to the car park, but more interesting is to leave just beyond a water-treatment plant through a gap in the right-hand wall. Drop through trees to a bridge and climb to a junction. Turn left, initially walking high above **Marcross Brook**, but later dropping to alternate between the banks over **stepping-stones** and shortly meeting the coast path at a bridge. You can follow the stream down to the beach or climb left back up to the car park, where the **tea cabin** is renowned for its Welsh cakes, to complete the walk. ♦

The Nash lighthouses

The twin lighthouses at Nash were built after the paddle steamer Frolic foundered off Nash Sands in 1831 with the loss of 78 passengers and crew. It took just 17 months to design, build and commission the lights to aid safe navigation past the shoal. Conversion to a single light in the 1920s left the western tower redundant, but the eastern light continues today under automatic operation. The light is open on weekend afternoons throughout the summer.

The distinctive, layered limestone cliffs at Col-huw

Llantwit Major

This enjoyable walk combines the ancient town of Llantwit Major with an invigorating stretch of cliffs and a fine beach

Distance/time: 6.5 km/4 miles. Allow 1½ to 2 hours

Start: Llantwit Major, car park behind the Old Town Hall (pay and display)

Grid ref: SS 967 687

Map: Ordnance Survey Explorer 151 (Cardiff & Bridgend)

After the walk: Old White Hart, Wine St, Llantwit Major CF61 1RZ | 01446 796809 OR Old Swan Inn, Church St, Llantwit Major CF61 1SB (by the car park in the village centre) | 01446 792230

Walk outline

The walk begins with a wander around the town's ancient church before heading across the fields to the coast past the site of a medieval monastery. Swinging along the coast, the route soon drops to the beach at the foot of Cwm Col-huw before climbing back to the cliffs past the embankments of an Iron Age coastal fort. Returning across fields, the way finishes along quiet back streets into the old town.

Llantwit Major

Llantwit's origins can be traced to the establishment of a seat of learning during the last decades of Roman rule in Britain, which was refounded as a monastic college in the 6th century by St Illtud.

The present church stands on the site of his simple chapel and contains ancient memorial stones from the 9th- and 10th- centuries, as well at 15th-century wall paintings. With access to a safe landing, the place prospered during the early medieval periods, with a manor court and even a coin mint — housed in what is now the Old Swan Inn.

Surfing at Col-huw

Kestrel

The Walk

1. Leave the car park beside the **Old Town Hall** and walk left past the **Old Swan Inn** and **Old White Hart**. Approaching the eastern end of the **church**, turn left and then go right beside the churchyard. Where the lane then bends right, keep ahead up steps to meet a track at the top.

2. Go left past cottages, leaving almost immediately over a stile on the right into a field. Strike diagonally left, passing a **dovecote**. Exit over a stile in the far corner onto a hedged track, **Church Lane** and follow it ahead to climb gently. Eventually after ½ mile/800 metres, the track enters the corner of a field. Carry on by the left hedge to a stile in the corner, from which a path falls along a shallow gully to the coast.

3. Climb away to the left along the coast path. After later crossing a stile, bear right at a fork, the path winding down to the head of the beach (**café** and **toilets**).

4. Cross the **Afon Col-huw** as it spills to the sea and walk through a **car park**. At the far end, climb away on a stepped path. Reaching a junction, go right to an impressive **viewpoint** from which the path swings left to continue along the cliff edge. Shortly, stiles mark the boundaries of an **Iron Age coastal fort**, its well-defined ramparts enclosing a large triangular area. The way continues beyond, cliff-top bushes now intermittently obscuring the view. Approaching a redundant stile, look for a path off to the left, which is the way back. However it is worth first wandering a little further to **Stout Point** for the view.

The Old Swan Inn at the heart of Llantwit Major

5. Return past the redundant stile and follow the field-edge from the cliffs, the way later becoming an enclosed track leading to **Rosedew Farm**. Through a gate, leave ahead along the farm lane to a junction. Turn right towards the town, shortly keeping ahead at a mini-roundabout.

6. Keep on past houses for another ¼ mile/400 metres to a junction and turn left along **Flanders Road**. Over a stream, the lane swings sharply left. Abandon it at that point, following the track ahead to **Flanders Farm**. Over a stile at the top, continue up steps into a field. Carry on by the right boundary to leave near the top corner by the **dovecote**. Retrace your outward steps into town to complete the walk. ◆

Col-huw

In the days when travel was often easier by sea than over land, the shingle beach at the foot of the Col-huw valley served as a landing for the scholastic settlement and abbey grange at Llantwit. Old documents record grain and other produce being shipped around the coast and across the channel to Bristol and Somerset. However, the small port was subsequently abandoned in the 16th century after it was destroyed by a ferocious storm.

Porthkerry's Grade II listed viaduct carries the railway to Cardiff

Porthkerry Country Park

A woodland walk around the old Porthkerry country estate, with an opportunity to explore the beach below the cliffs

What to expect:
Country park and woodland paths with a couple of steep climbs

Distance/time: 6.5 km/4 miles. Allow 2 to 2½ hours

Start: Porthkerry Country Park Forest Café car park (charge summer Sundays and bank holidays)

Grid ref: ST 086 668

Map: Ordnance Survey Explorer 151 (Cardiff & Bridgend)

After the walk: Forest Café (by car park), Porthkerry Park CF62 3BY | 01446 739209 OR Toby Carvery, Port Road West, Rhoose CF62 3BA (on A4226 towards airport) | 01446 700075

Walk outline

Beginning at the heart of the country park, the walk is one of ups and downs, climbing to the old hamlet of Porthkerry, then dropping to Lower Porthkerry, only to climb again over the farmed headland of West Ridge. Back in the valley, the route takes you up and down the wooded fold of Cwm Cidi before returning along the main valley to the car park.

Porthkerry Park

Porthkerry Park was laid out in the 1840s by the Romilly family, who ran the estate as a model farm, building cottages for their workers and a sawmill to process timber from the surrounding woodlands. The woods cloaking the steeper slopes by Golden Stairs, however, have never been managed and are considered to be truly ancient.

Thinning of the tree canopy, initially for the benefit of primroses, has led to an increase in the rare greater butterfly orchid. Today, as many as 300 tall, butterfly-like flower spikes can be seen in summer. Other rarities found at Porthkerry include bird's-nest orchids and glow worms.

12-hole golf course

Glow worm

The Walk

1. Leaving the car park, walk towards the coast. Just past the golf hut, cross a bridge onto the **golf course** and, keeping a wary eye open for flying golf balls, cross to a break in the trees opposite. Bear right, climbing steeply to a fork. Take the left branch and carry on uphill beside an old iron fence. Emerging from the wood at the top, follow a gravel drive to the right into **Porthkerry**.

Despite sitting above a short railway tunnel and just beyond the eastern end of Cardiff Airport's main runway, the little hamlet of Porthkerry appears lost in the heart of the Welsh countryside. At its centre stands a simple whitewashed church,

dedicated to St Curig, a 6th-century bishop of Llanbadarn and Brittany. Although quite Victorianised inside, the building was erected in the 13th century, probably on the site of a much older chapel. In the graveyard is a medieval preaching cross from the 15th century.

2. Beyond **St Curig's Church**, branch off right along the back edge of a small green and past a house. Continue on a descending path into wood. Breaking from the trees at the bottom, walk on at the edge of hay meadow to the end of a lane.

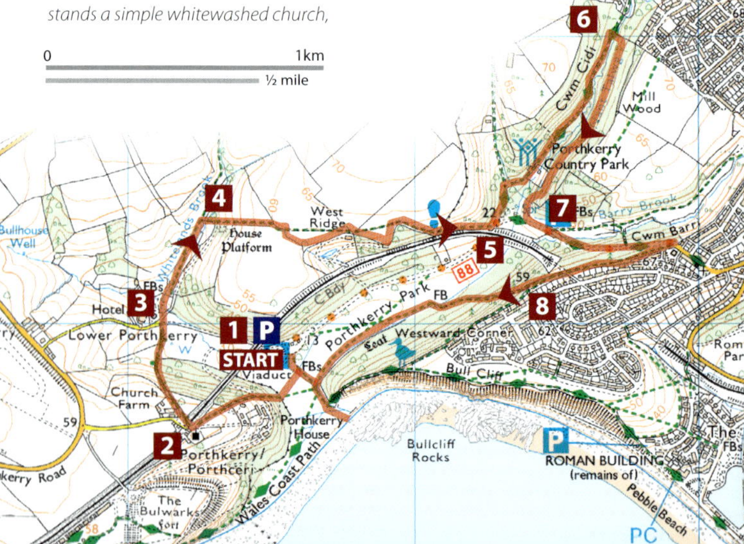

Recreational cyclists speed towards Porthkerry's distinctive viaduct

3. Go left and immediately right into more trees. Crossing a bridge, a broader track soon leads to a stile into pasture. Walk up the gentle valley fold, slipping over a field bridge to continue with **Whitelands Brook** now on your right. Over a double stile at the top keep going for another 100 metres to a stile on the right.

4. Back in woodland, recross the stream and climb away past a ruined building to come out into another field. Strike ahead to a stile in the top corner and carry on by the left hedge to a gate. Walk right, skirting two sides of the field to a stile in the corner by a house. Pass through a small of copse and continue with the right boundary to a stile at the indented corner of the wood. A path descends into the trees, curving at the bottom beside a **railway line** and eventually emerging beside a bridge onto the park drive.

5. Walk left to a bend, there leaving ahead along a track. Soon reaching a fork, branch right through a gate and follow a track into **Cwm Cidi**. Keep

Passenger trains still rumble across Porthkerry viaduct

going for almost ½ mile/800 metres, eventually reaching a gate at the top.

The sawmill at the foot of Cwm Cidi was built in 1835 to handle timber produced on the estate and worked by three generations of sawmen until the estate was bought by the local authority in 1929. The building was then used as a scout hut before finally being abandoned.

Standing two storeys high, the mill was powered by a cast iron breast-shot wheel and incorporated a saw bench on the ground floor with a wood turning lathe upstairs. The millpond on the hill just behind was fed by two long leats bringing water from both Nant Tawlg and Barri Brook.

6. Instead of passing through, drop right across the **brook** to pick up a rough path returning down the other side of the valley. Eventually reaching a junction, keep ahead with red and yellow markers, to emerge from the trees by a **car park**.

7. Follow the main drive left, climbing along **Cwm Barri**. Leaving the park, turn right along **Coed yr Odyn**. Keep ahead as it swings left to garages, passing a terrace of houses and continuing along the top edge of **Cliff Wood**.

8. Reaching a fork, bear right, descending along **Lovers Lane** into the valley. Just past the **ruin of Cliffwood Cottage**, cross a bridge over **Nant Tawlg** and follow the stream on to meet a path at the corner of the wood. The car park is to the right — but you might first want to go left to the **beach** — to complete the walk. ♦

Long lost tree?

Some of the steeper slopes in Porthkerry Woods hold ancient woodland. A surprising discovery in 1983 was a single true service tree, which is known in only a handful of sites across Britain. Some 80 plants have since been identified across the estate and work is being undertaken to preserve its habitat, including the removal of holm oaks. With long pinnate leaves (similar to a rowan) and pear shaped fruits, the tree can live for over 400 years.

An old-fashioned merry-go-round contrasts with modern architecture at Cardiff Bay

Cardiff Bay

Cardiff Bay is a bold symbol of regeneration in Wales and a focus for art, culture and leisure in the country's capital city

Distance/time: 9.5 km/6 miles. Allow 2½ to 3 hours

Start: Cardiff Bay Barrage car park at Penarth (pay and display)

Grid ref: ST 190 724

Map: Ordnance Survey Explorer 151 (Cardiff & Bridgend)

After the walk: Wide choice of bars, restaurants, cafés and coffee houses at the head of the bay

Walk outline

Beginning across the locks of the Barrage, the walk follows the eastern shore of Cardiff Bay to the Pierhead by the National Assembly building and the Wales Millennium Centre. The route carries on around the bay, passing a wetland reserve before crossing the River Taff. The way continues past the Ice Centre, International Pool and White Water flume before crossing the River Ely. A promenade takes the last leg past a waterfront village, finally cutting back across the foot of a marina.

Cardiff Bay

The docks at Penarth and Cardiff were once amongst the busiest in the world, shipping coal, iron and other goods across the Empire. Tonnage peaked at the start of the 20th century, but despite the busyness created by two World Wars, their trade gradually declined and by the early 1970s, much of the infrastructure was becoming derelict. The renaissance began in 1987 with work on the Barrage and regeneration of docklands around the bay. Today, a 200-hectare freshwater lake extends over the old tidal mudflats, overlooked by developments that put business, and leisure side by side in the heart of Wales' first city.

The 'Norwegian Church'

Mute swans

The Walk

1. Cross the **Barrage** to follow a path above the shore that leads to a white canopy sheltering a display commemorating Scott's embarkation from Cardiff en route to the South Pole in 1910. Further along, another small exhibition celebrates the Welsh coal industry. Continue beside the waterfront past a **graving dock** to a mini roundabout.

The Barrage was a controversial development, not least because it would result in the flooding of a massive area of tidal mudflats surrounding the estuaries of the Taff and Ely, a perennial feeding ground for thousands of waders and seabirds. The creation of the Newport Wetlands RSPB Reserve (featured in Walk 9) was intended to mitigate some of this crucial habitat loss, as was the formation of a smaller wetland reserve at the edge of Cardiff Bay. Following a period of transition as the reedbeds adapted from a saltwater to a freshwater environment, the installation of a fish ladder beside the Barrage allows

salmon and trout to migrate into the rivers to breed.

2. Swing left, passing the **Doctor Who Experience**, behind which is the **World of Boats**. Over a bridge spanning the foot of **Roath Basin**, carry on past the **Norwegian Church Arts Centre** towards Y Senedd, the **Welsh National Assembly building**. Just beyond is the **Pierhead Building**, built in 1897 as the headquarters for the Bute Dock

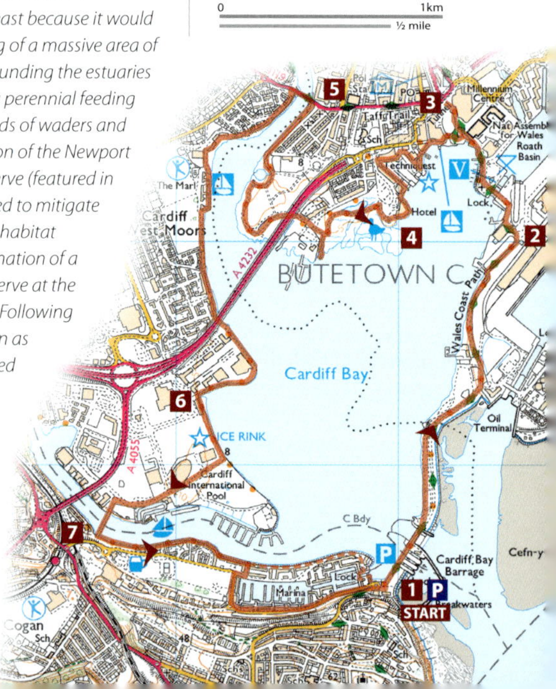

Cardiff Bay's Millennium Centre is an architectural masterpiece

Company, with **Roald Dahl Plass** and the **Wales Millennium Centre** behind.

The sunken plaza behind the Pierhead Building commemorates Roald Dahl, who was born in Cardiff to Norwegian parents in 1916 and christened in the White Church, now an arts centre. The Plass occupies the site of the basin to the infilled West Bute Dock, while nearby is a statue to the Cardiff-born popular composer and actor Ivor Novello. Overlooking all is the Wales Millennium Centre, an arts and theatre complex which also houses the tourist information centre.

3. Return to the **Pierhead** and go right over the foot of **Roald Dahl Plass**, following the waterfront past the **Mermaid Quay** complex and **Landsea Gardens**. Turn in around the **Mount Stuart graving docks** and swing left along **Sovereign Quay** towards **St David's Hotel**, where a wooden walkway takes the route around the building. (Adverse weather can close the walkway, in which case pass around the landward side of the building.)

4. The path then winds through a **wetland nature reserve**, where a

An eclectic mix of old and new buildings enliven Cardiff Bay

duckboard leads out to a viewing platform. Return and continue with the main path to a mini-roundabout. Keep ahead beneath the main road, skirting **Harmadrayd Park** beside the **River Taff**. Leaving the park, walk on along **Clarence Embankment** to the main road.

5. Turn left over the bridge, dropping left again on the far bank by a zebra crossing. Head downstream with the riverside path, coming out opposite the **Water Activity Centre**. Go left, bearing left again in front of **The Sand Wharf** apartments to resume the riverside path.

Walk on beneath the road bridge and skirt the **International Sports Village**.

6. Approaching a road, swing left with a waterside boardwalk, leaving after 200 metres at a signpost to the swimming pool. Reaching a roundabout, keep ahead past **White Water International** and a boat park compound before turning off left along a **cycleway** onto **Pont Y Werin** across the **River Ely**.

7. On the south bank go left beside the road. A waterfront promenade leads all the way round to the mouth of the **Portway Marin**a, but if the lock is in use, you cannot cross and may have to double back around the two dock basins. The alternative is to leave the promenade after ¼ mile/400 metres along **Jeffcott Place** to the main street. Go right and then left along **Penarth Portway**, keeping left again at a mini roundabout. Follow the road back to the car park by the Barrage to complete the walk. ♦

Wildlife in the bay

Dragonflies dart above the water, while insect and fish larvae are food for birds and a surprising range of species visit or breed around the wetland reserve. Tufted ducks, coots, swans and cormorants may be seen at any time of year, while winter visitors include stonechat, teal and water rail. Kingfishers and herons are often on the lookout for a meal and reed bunting and sedge warblers nest amongst the reeds.

Dense reedbeds provide precious habitat for warblers, bearded tits and bitterns

Nash & Uskmouth

Explore the coastal bird life from the Newport Wetlands RSPB Reserve

Distance/time: 9 km/5½ miles. Allow 2 to 2½ hours

Start: Newport Wetlands RSPB Reserve car park

Grid ref: ST 334 834

Map: Ordnance Survey Explorer 152 (Newport & Pontypool)

After the walk: Café at visitor centre NP18 2BZ | 01633 636363 OR Waterloo Inn, West Nash Road, Nash NP18 2BZ | 01633 274525

Walk outline

After skirting the northern perimeter of the reserve the walk follows the flood defences overlooking the tidal marshes beside the mouth of the River Severn. Later, leaving the coast, old tracks and quiet lanes take the route inland to Nash, where the Waterloo Inn serves food. The way back to the reserve lies across old grazing meadows, picking a serpentine course to find bridges across the innumerable reens.

Newport Wetlands RSPB Reserve

Extending over some 437 hectares, the reserve was established in 2000 by the RSPB in partnership with Natural Resources Wales and Newport City Council to mitigate the loss of wetlands caused by the creation of Cardiff Bay. Although including areas of farmland reclaimed from the Caldicote Levels, much of the site was formerly a tip used for the disposal of fuel ash from the nearby power station.

Incorporated within the reserve is a complex of reens, saline lagoons, reedbeds and wet grasslands, with saltmarsh and mudflats occupying the intertidal zone beside the Usk estuary. Located near the entrance to the reserve is an informative visitor centre and café.

East Usk lighthouse

Bearded tit

The Walk

1. Before starting the walk, you might first visit the **RSPB visitor centre** to find out what wildlife has recently been spotted on the reserve. It lies a short distance along **Perry Lane**, behind the car park.

Return to the **car park** and go left to find a path signed to 'Goldcliff' leaving by a larger-than-life reed mace. At a junction, swing left along the fringe of wetland scrub. Keep with the main track, ignoring paths off left into the reserve. Eventually, wind beneath power cables to reach the coast.

Attracting migrants as well as providing a variety of habitats for residents, over 150 different species of birds have been recorded at Newport Wetlands. Spring heralds the breeding season when swifts and swallows arrive from sub-Saharan Africa, darting through the air to pick insects off the wing. As the year segues into summer, there is a frenzy of feeding and the young birds take to the air, building stamina for the long journey south. Autumn and winter, however, are often considered the 'best' times for estuarine marshes. Migrating birds heading back south such as wheatear, redstart and willow warbler might pause to refuel, while others like ruff, dunlin, curlew and oystercatcher arrive to spend winter feeding on the marshes or mudflats.

2. To the left, the way continues along the top of the **sea defences** overlooking a coastal fringe of saltmarsh grazing

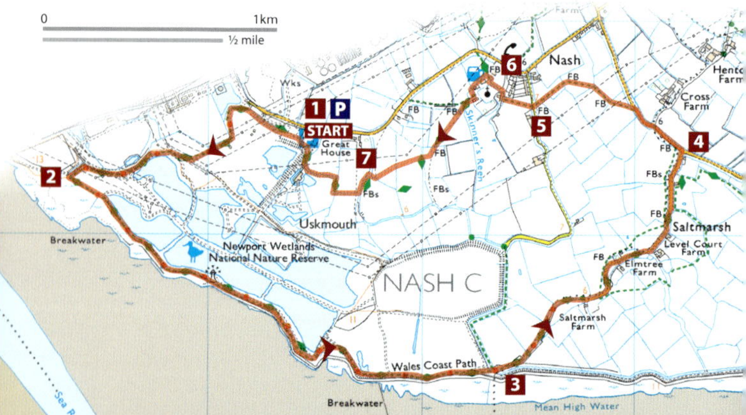

An informative visitor centre at the heart of the Newport Wetlands

and mud, which is exposed at low tide. After ½ mile/800 metres, you reach the **East Usk lighthouse**, which continues to operate as a navigation marker for vessels entering the **River Usk**.

Erected in 1893, East Usk Lighthouse complemented the already existing western light to guide shipping into the mouth of the River Usk. It was the first Trinity House light to incorporate the Dalén Sun Valve, a device that automatically switched on and ignited the gas supply as darkness fell. Used with a device to make the light flash, the invention dramatically

reduced gas consumption, allowing the light to operate unmanned for a full year on 12 cylinders of gas. The light was eventually converted to electricity in 1972.

Carry on with the coast path, ignoring the first path off left, but then bending sharply left a little further on. Take the first right to resume with the coast, walking for another ½ mile/800 metres before dropping from the sea wall to a junction.

3. Bear left (not hard left), the way soon becoming tree-lined beside a reen. Emerging beside a cottage at **Saltmarsh Farm**, continue along **Saltmarsh Lane**.

East Usk lighthouse helps guide tankers in the busy Usk estuary

4. At the end, go left along **Goldcliff Road**.

After ¼ mile/400 metres, just around a bend, look for a sign indicating a footpath leaving over a stile beside a gate on the left. Strike three-quarters right across lush meadow to a gated bridge and then keep ahead by the right hedge, passing through the corner into another field. Head across to another bridge, halfway along the left boundary, and continue ahead along the length of the field to come out onto a narrow lane.

5. Cross to the bridge opposite and bear right across a final meadow towards the **church**. Leave through a kissing gate tucked in the right corner and walk out to a street. Bear left, passing between the churchyard and a children's playing field to the **Waterloo Inn**.

6. At the bend just before the pub, keep ahead to find a stiled bridge at the back of the parking area. Turn left behind the pub to a bridge and carry on beside the winding reen to another bridge in the corner. Strike across the next pasture to find a crossing in the far-right corner. Walk forward to a gated bridge on the left, over which head away by the left boundary.

After crossing two bridges, swing right beside a reen and keep going over more bridges until you emerge onto a track.

7. Go left for 150 metres then leave through kissing gates on the right. A grass track winds away between the ditches to emerge on **Perry Lane** beside the **Newport Wetlands reserve** and its **visitor centre**. The car park is then just to the right, to complete the walk. ◆

'Murmurations' of starlings

A spectacular sight over the reserve in winter is huge numbers of starlings, which gather at dusk in murmurations or flocks numbering 60,000 or more. When the conditions are right they take to the sky in seemingly orchestrated displays in which the whole flock twist and weave in a truly beautiful aerial ballet, the air noisy with their chatter. Then, just as dramatically, they can disappear as they settle en-masse into the reeds to roost for the night.

A high embankment helps protect the low-lying Gwent Levels from flooding

Redwick

A walk on the coastal levels, reclaimed from the sea by the monks of Goldcliff Priory during the 15th century

What to expect:
Coastal and field paths, some tracks, metal bridge crossing pipeline not suitable for dogs

Distance/time: 8 km/5 miles. Allow 2 to 2½ hours

Start: Lay by on Porton Road in Whitson, west of church

Grid ref: ST 379 834

Map: Ordnance Survey Explorer 152 (Newport & Pontypool)

After the walk: The Rose Inn, South Row, Redwick NP26 3DU | 01633 880501

Walk outline

Beginning at the tiny hamlet of Whitson, the walk makes for the coast at Porton House, climbing onto the flood defences as it continues beside the saltmarshes bordering the Mouth of the River Severn. Turning inland, field paths lead to Redwick, an engaging village with an interesting church, quirky outdoors 'museum' and a welcoming pub. The walk back across the fields to Redwick follows the line of a medieval way.

Whitson and Redwick

With one of the highest tidal ranges in the world, it is hardly surprising to learn that the Gwent Levels were once an extensive saltmarsh, regularly inundated by the sea.

The Romans were the first to begin reclaiming land from the tide for farming, but it was the efforts of the monastic landlords of Goldcliff and Tintern that really created the basis for the landscape we see today. Both Whitson and Redwick date from this period, serving as a focus for scattered farms and cider orchards. But, with much of the land lying below sea level at high tide, maintenance of the flood defences and drainage systems remains a demanding, never-ending activity.

Cider press, Redwick

Curlew

The Walk

1. Go south along the lane, following it left around a sharp bend. After 250 metres, turn off through a gate immediately in front of a farm shed on the right. Walk through to the meadow beyond and cross to a gate at the far side. Over a grass track, continue straight ahead across the next two fields.

Entering the third field, go left beside the ditch to a stile in the corner. Cross another track and bridge then swing right beside the reen. Over another bridge, make a bee-line towards **Porton House**, crossing the intervening track to rejoin it by the house. Turn right over a gated bridge and climb onto the **flood embankment**.

2. Walk left through a gate and follow the seawall, later crossing a pipeline that drains water from the Llanwern Steelworks to the sea.

Carry on for another ¾ mile/1.2 kilometres eventually approaching a track rising from below by **Windmill Reen** and its sluice below the flood embankment.

3. Drop back left to the bottom track and cross a bridge into the adjacent field. Follow the perimeter right, turning within the corner to walk on up the field edge past a sluice gate to another bridge. Cross and turn through a gate immediately on the left.

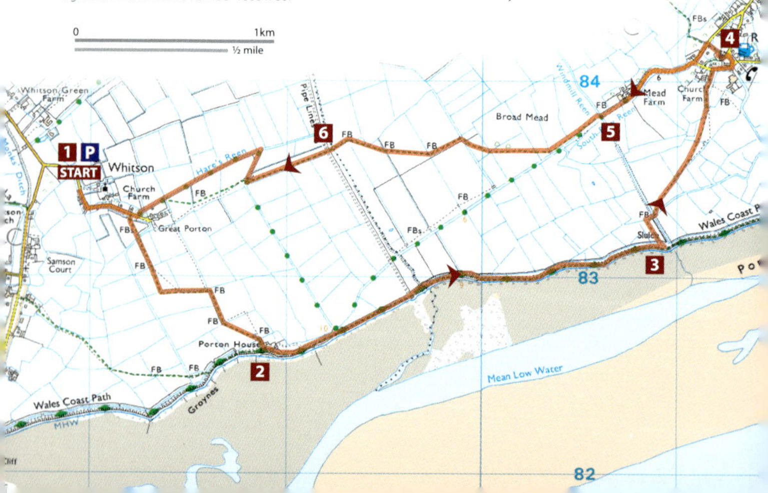

The unusual, Grade I listed church of St Thomas at Redwick

Strike half-right towards the church tower to find a gated bridge partway along the boundary (not the field gate a little further left) and continue with the right hedge. In the next field carry on to a bridge in the far boundary, maintaining the line beyond to a gate just left of a tree. Follow the hedge past a farm to emerge onto a lane in **Redwick**. Turn right to a junction opposite **The Rose Inn**. The **village 'museum'** and **church** are then to the left.

The shelter beside the road is modern, but is constructed of old stones found in the vicinity, and contains many curiosities from the old farming life of the village such as mill and press stones, field rollers and shafts from ancient preaching crosses. The ancient orchards surrounding the village provided apples for cider-making and there is a restored apple crusher and cider press.

4. Leave the northern edge of the graveyard over a stile and follow a leafy path to come out onto a lane. Go left to a junction and keep ahead along the aptly-named **Mead Lane**.

The remnants of old fish traps jut from the Severn Estuary's tidal mudflats

5. Beyond **Mead Farm**, cross a bridge and immediately leave over stile beside a gate on the right. Following 'Redwick Circular Walk' signs, keep with the left hedge into the third field and then bear right to another bridge. Maintain the same general easterly heading from field to field, eventually reaching the **Llanwern pipeline**.

6. Cross a **high metal bridge** to a track. Go left and almost immediately pass through a gate on the right and head out along another field. At the far end, swing right on a green track. Reaching a junction, walk left, eventually passing through trees to emerge on the lane in **Whitson**. Turn right back to the lay by near **St Thomas' Church** to complete the walk.

Founded in the 12th century, the original dedication to St Michael was changed after the Dissolution of the monasteries by Henry VIII. St Thomas' Church is one of the largest in the area and unusual in having an immersion baptistry pool that can fill naturally with water after heavy rain.

The Victorian painted glass in the east window is all that remains after the church was badly damaged when bombs fell on the village from a stray Luftwaffe bomber in August 1942. One cottage was destroyed and several others damaged, while the church lost most of its roof and windows and remained closed until 1949. As you leave, look in the porch for a mark showing the level to which the water rose during the Great Flood of 1607, while in the graveyard are the remains of a medieval preaching cross; a truncated shaft set in the original socket. ♦

Mistletoe

Many of the trees passed along the way contain clumps of mistletoe, particularly obvious during the winter when they appear as green, leafy balls high amongst the otherwise bare branches. Appearing to grow almost magically upon other trees, it is steeped in folklore. Sprigs were hung above doorways to protect against storm and other evils, while the berries, although toxic, were a miraculous cure-all and powerful aphrodisiac.

Useful Information

Wales Coast Path

Comprehensive information about all sections of the Wales Coast Path can be found at **www.walescoastpath.gov.uk**

Visit South Wales

The South Wales official tourism website covers everything from accommodation and special events to attractions and adventure. **www.visitwales.com/explore/south-wales**

Tourist Information and National Park Centres

The main TICs provide free information on everything from accommodation and transport to what's on and walking advice.

Swansea	01792 468 321	tourism@swansea.gov.uk
Porthcawl	01656 786 639	porthcawltic@bridgend.gov.uk
Bridgend	01656 654 906	bridgendtic@bridgend.gov.uk
Barry Island	01446 747 171	barrytic@valeofglamorgan.gov.uk
Cardiff	029 20873 573	visitor@cardiff.gov.uk
Newport	01633 842 962	newport.tic@newport.gov.uk
Chepstow	01291 623 772	chepstow.tic@monmouthshire.gov.uk

Weather

Online weather forecasts for South Wales are available from the Met Office at **www.metoffice.gov.uk**

Rail Travel

Main railway stations are located at Swansea, Port Talbot, Bridgend, Barry, Cardiff, Newport and Chepstow.

Information is available from National Rail Enquiries on 03457 484950 or **www.nationalrail.co.uk**

Bus Travel

The main towns and many of the villages are served by bus services.

Traveline Cymru - 0871 200 22 33 - **www.travelinecymru.info,**

www.firstgroup.com/ukbus/south_west_wales/